About the Author

Mezzo-soprano Sophia Grech is an internationally acclaimed opera singer with a career spanning over two decades having graduated from the Royal College of Music in 1995. She has been featured and reviewed in the world's press including national newspapers and magazines, having also given television and radio interviews.

She has won great acclaim and notoriety for her performances at leading concert halls, opera houses and international festivals worldwide, leading to regular invitations to give masterclasses around the world.

In 2015 Sophia was diagnosed with autism and is now a leading Ambassador on behalf of associated organisations alongside her performing career.

For more information about the author, and her career, visit:
www.mezzo-soprano-sophia-grech.co.uk

I Wish I Could Sing

Sophia Grech

I Wish I Could Sing

Olympia Publishers

London

www.olympiapublishers.com

OLYMPIA PAPERBACK EDITION

A CIP catalogue record for this title is
available from the British Library.

ISBN: 978-1-78830-693-5

First Published in 2020

Olympia Publishers
Tallis House
2 Tallis Street
London
EC4Y 0AB

Printed in Great Britain

Dedication

In memory of Avril Elizabeth Grech, my lovely mum, who supported me throughout my career and who always wanted to improve her singing alongside her love of music.

Acknowledgements

I would like to thank the following people for their support in the composition of my book. My father John Grech for the cartoon artwork, Rene Lawson for the diagram illustrations, photographer Ellissia Grech, other family and friends namely Andy Dickinson and Diane Day. I would also like to thank Olympia Publishers for investing in and supporting the publication of my book.

Contents

'The voice is an instrument we all have and which we are all born with. Singing is a self–expression we all use whether in the bathroom or on the concert stage, no matter how your voice sounds, respect it, as each one is unique.'

Sophia Grech

Introduction

The voice is the oldest and most natural of all instruments and the desire to experience the feeling of making a musical sound dates back to the Stone Age.

Regardless of your age, gender or physical abilities, this simple guide will help you to improve both your voice and your confidence to sing. Singing can feel embarrassing for most people, but this is only because you don't know what to do physically when you sing, so you end up feeling nervous and unconfident as if being asked to do something highly embarrassing. In the lessons that follow, you will learn how to use your body to help you sing correctly, how to stand, how to breathe and use your face to help you control and produce a better sound.

A musical background is not necessary, but the enthusiasm to improve your ability to sing is essential. The lessons are unbelievably easy to follow; there are no music scores to struggle with or complicated CDs to listen to. It is so simple and straightforward you will be surprised how much you will learn about singing and how easy some of the technique is. You will be amazed at how much your singing will improve; however, it is important to understand that progress in singing will vary from individual to individual, as no two people are alike. Natural vocal ability together with endurance, imagination and personality, all contribute to the end result.

So why did I write these lessons?

There is no doubt that singing is the strangest 'instrument' to teach, as the voice is invisible. A good singing teacher should possess a sound technical foundation and a lively imagination. Throughout my 25 years of performing and teaching, I have condensed and developed a number of difficult techniques into easy, simple and effective methods that everyone can manage. These methods are so easy that learning and developing good singing techniques will feel like fun!

For those who don't have access to a good teacher, or who do not want to take singing lessons, I will teach you the basic principles needed to begin to improve your voice. With practice and concentration, everyone should feel the benefit from the guidance and advice contained within the lessons. In order to sing to the best of your ability, whether you choose to sing pop, musical theatre, classical, opera, jazz or folk songs, the basic techniques are the same. So, what is a good technique? It is simply the accumulation of good habits ('good singing' is 'good habits').

Each of the lessons concentrates on the important aspects of singing. For these lessons to become 'good habits', you must take the time to refine each technique, ensuring you feel comfortable with it before moving onto the next. Follow the simple step-by-step exercises to feel and hear an improvement in your voice. As you work your way through the lessons, your range will expand and you will be able to sing higher; your voice will become louder and you will be able to sing in tune. You might also experience other benefits such as 'vibrato' (the natural wobble in the voice) for some people this is natural, others need time for it to develop and for the rest, it might never come! Don't worry; you don't need vibrato to enjoy singing!

At the end of each lesson, you can apply and repeat what you have learnt by singing along to your favourite CD or karaoke backing track, or you may choose to sing alone with no musical accompaniment. Whatever you choose to sing is up to you as long as you are comfortable and enjoy the song.

As you work through the lessons, look out for my 'top tips' and recommended daily practice times.

'Have fun!'

Lesson One:
Your Body

'Oh no… don't put your hands behind your back!'

Time and time again I see people singing with their hands behind their backs, clutching them together as if they were some incredible aid that they could not sing without.

From their first day at school, many children are taught to sing with their hands behind their backs because it looks tidy! Singing with your hands behind your back can be a damaging habit if continued for many years, as it pulls and strains the body in all the wrong places; try to remember, although it looks tidy and may feel comfortable, it is a hindrance and not a help.

How you stand and prepare your body is the first step to improving your voice, try to imagine your voice as an instrument. You must prepare it before you play it; for example, you can't play an electric keyboard if it's not plugged in!

For some people standing for long periods may feel uncomfortable, especially if you suffer from back pain or any other physical problems. Don't worry, as this will not affect your singing.

Follow the exercises below:

If you are unable to stand for the exercises, practise them sitting down instead.

Exercise 1.

Stand naturally with your hands by your side, don't clamp your arms tightly against your body; try to create some space between your arms and body.

If you prefer, you can hold your hands in front of you: whatever feels more comfortable. If you are sitting down, then rest your hands in your lap by either putting them on your knees or holding your hands together.

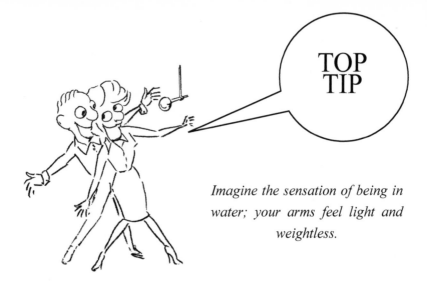

Imagine the sensation of being in water; your arms feel light and weightless.

Exercise 2.

Stand up straight with your shoulders back and your chest out, as though you are feeling very proud.

Exercise 3.

When you are standing correctly, remember to keep breathing (you might feel the need to hold your breath). Standing in this position may feel uncomfortable at first, but try to relax.

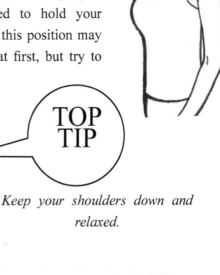

Keep your shoulders down and relaxed.

Exercise 4.

Stand with your feet slightly apart so that your weight is evenly distributed. You can stand with one foot slightly in front of the other for comfort, if you wish. Feel your weight evenly distributed so you feel strong and steady on your feet. Keep your legs straight, but relax your knees occasionally to stop you from tensing up. Never stand with your feet together.

It is important to rehearse the above exercises; they will help your body to become a strong frame from which you can begin to sing.

Exercise 5.

Now, standing correctly, play a CD and sing along to your favourite songs. You can also use a backing track or sing unaccompanied if you prefer.

Recommended daily practice: as long as you feel comfortable, you can practise the exercises for as long as you feel necessary.

TOP TIP

Stand in front of a mirror, preferably full-length, and repeat what you have learnt. Take note of how you look and try to remember how it feels.

In the next lesson, you will learn how to breathe correctly for singing and how to improve your breath intake.

Lesson Two:
Breathing

Please note, this lesson is more suitable for adults and teenagers and must be limited for young children; however, encouragement to take a 'big breath' is fine.

In order to make the most of your singing ability, I will teach you how to increase your capacity for air intake, which will in turn, strengthen the muscles that will enable you to breathe properly. As your breathing improves, you will gain more stamina and this in turn will increase your vocal strength.

Breathing for singing is similar to normal breathing, the movement is the same, but it's more exaggerated and deeper. When singing, it is very important that you always breathe through your mouth and not your nose.

There are two stages when learning to breathe for singing,

the first uses your chest and the second uses your diaphragm. This lesson will cover just the first stage of breathing with your chest, breathing from the diaphragm is not hard to learn, but applying it to singing is more advanced and should not be attempted at this stage.

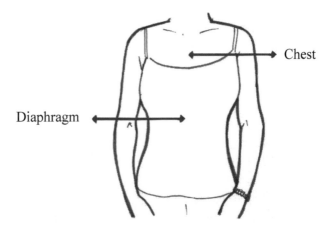

The simple motion of breathing is one of the most important technical requirements in singing. By breathing in, you prepare to support your voice, and by breathing out you 'play' the voice, or make a sound, because we can all breathe, we can all sing! Some simply have a better natural capacity than others, but we can all improve. Follow this lesson carefully, as it will form the foundation of the technique you need to realise the potential of your singing voice.

Using the information from the previous lesson, stand correctly, preferably in front of a mirror, and check your posture. When you are satisfied you are ready, begin the breathing exercises.

Exercise 1.

Put one hand on your chest and take a deep breath, as you do so lift your chest up (you should see your chest rise) then breathe out and watch it relax. Practise this a few times, working hard at each attempt – breathe as though you are about to go underwater; it is important to remember to breathe through your mouth.

Please note that deep breathing can cause dizziness, or may cause you to feel faint. If this occurs stop the exercise and come back to it later.

Exercise 2.

Keeping one hand on your chest, put your other hand lower down on your stomach. Take a slow deep breath, lifting your chest and feel how your stomach moves naturally.

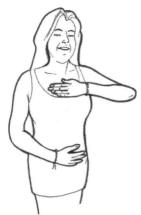

Repeat this a few times with your eyes closed so you can concentrate on how it feels.

Exercise 3.

Practise the above exercise and watch yourself in the mirror. Make sure your shoulders only lift a natural amount, ensuring that you don't lift them too high! Be careful not to tense or 'suck in' your neck muscles.

If you experience a lack of movement in your chest when you breathe, don't worry, it can take a few weeks to improve.

TOP TIP

Try to memorise how your good habits feel then step away from the mirror and repeat them.

When to breathe during a song?

Breathing is a natural bodily function; as such, you don't need to think about when or where to breathe. When you speak, taking a breath occurs naturally without having to consciously think about it; this is a natural pause before you continue talking. It is the same for singing, you can feel when you need to breathe; look at the words of a song and you will see the commas and full stops.

The trick is, don't wait until you have physically run out of air before you take another breath, this makes the song sound unnatural and you will feel exhausted; after all, you don't do this when you speak. So instead of struggling to make it to the end of the phrase or sentence, just take a breath; however, avoid taking it in the middle of a word, as it will sound very unnatural.

Do I need to breathe quietly?

No! It is perfectly OK and natural to be heard taking a breath whilst singing. The intake of air needed for singing is much stronger than speaking, so you will and should be able to hear the air as you take a deep breath in.

Recommended daily practice: this depends on your age; too much deep breathing can make you feel dizzy so follow the guidelines below:

Under 10 years of age: limited to taking a 'big breath'.
Under 16 years of age: 2-5 minutes a few days a week.
Adults: 2-5 minutes a day for five days a week.

When you feel confident, sing along to your favourite songs and practise your breathing, also refer back to lesson 1 and remember to stand correctly with the right posture.

In the next lesson, I will teach you how to use your face to achieve a better sound, thus helping to control your voice, this will help you look and sound more like a singer. You will also learn how to use your face as an aide to help you sing higher.

Lesson Three:
Your Face

Your face is very important for singing, not just for the production of sound, but because it is the window of your self-expression. In this lesson, you will practise raising your face by 'smiling', 'looking surprised' and 'raising your eyebrows'.

When singing, your face must be lifted and your cheekbones raised. There are three facial expressions you can make to achieve this:

Smiling.

Looking surprised.

Raising your eyebrows.

Just these three simple actions can have the most dramatic effect on your voice. When you smile, your face lifts and your cheekbones rise, for maximum facial lift simply look surprised and raise your eyebrows! The effect this has on your voice will become evident almost immediately. Not only will it help you to sing higher, but also your sound quality will be much better.

The eyebrows are also very important to a singer; most of us continually lift and lower our eyebrows, often subconsciously, as a form of facial expression. However, deliberate raising of the eyebrows is, for many reasons, a useful tool for a singer; for example, it contributes to the facial lift and allows the expression of the eyes to be seen much more clearly. Surprisingly, it also helps you to reach the high notes more easily!

It is not necessary to raise your eyebrows constantly; however, as a beginner, you should be encouraged to do it as much as possible during the first six months, especially when singing higher.

Some people will find it difficult to raise their eyebrows, don't worry about this! Just by trying you will be benefiting.

Exercise 1.

Stand in front of the mirror, put your fingers on your cheekbones and smile (with your mouth open). Feel how your cheekbones lift up. Try to keep your head level and look straight ahead.

Exercise 2.

Now practise looking surprised! Try to remember how it feels when something happy surprises you, look in the mirror and with your eyebrows raised look surprised.

TOP
TIP

If you find your face is aching, don't worry, it means your muscles are working.

Exercise 3.

Check your posture, take a deep breath and whilst lifting your chest, lift your face at the same time – concentrate and practise each individual movement. It can be hard to do everything at once, but in time, you will become much quicker; more importantly, try not to become frustrated.

If you are singing a sad song, smiling may not look appropriate. However, you must still lift your face, which can be achieved by smiling just a little.

Recommended daily practice: 3-10 minutes for five days a week.
For children under 10 years of age, two days a week.

In the next lesson, you will practise your singing techniques whilst 'humming'.

Lesson Four: Humming

Humming is the first sound you should make when learning to sing. Professional singers often use humming as a form of warming up before giving a performance. It warms up your vocal functions and helps create resonance (a kind of buzzing sensation); it will also help your voice to focus and sit correctly.

TOP TIP

Humming will help you sing in tune.

For the following exercises use a well-known song, for example, 'Happy Birthday'.

Exercise 1.

With a slight smile and your lips touching lightly together, slowly start to hum the song. (Listen as to whether you sound in tune or not.) If your lips tingle uncomfortably, very slightly open your mouth.

Experiment by humming at different ranges of your voice, either higher or lower or until you find where it feels comfortable. You do not need to use a piano or any other musical device to find a note, simply pick where feels comfortable and that will be right.

Exercise 2.

Standing in front of your mirror check your posture. Take a deep breath (raising your chest) and lift your face with a 'smile' before humming the first line of the song, then repeat.

Exercise 3.

When you feel satisfied, try humming the whole song, experiment by humming it higher and lower.

Recommended daily practice: 3-10 minutes for five days a week.

For young children two days a week.

Now you are ready to sing!

Lesson Five:
Singing Words

Singing would be easier if we didn't have any words, but words are essential to make a song; they give the song meaning, emotion and communication. The problem is that certain words can be incredibly awkward to sing, this is due to the various mouth shapes you will make and how they can disturb the natural flow of the voice. The problem occurs because you need to keep your mouth open as much as possible for singing, think about it: if your mouth is closed, how can the sound come out? There is a simple solution to this problem, open your mouth wider! Another technique is to sing the consonants quicker and exaggerate them.

Exercise 1.

Practise saying various consonants: 'put pressure' on them, as if you are exaggerating and accentuating them with a strong pronunciation.

Say the following consonants out loud:

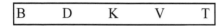

B   D   K   V   T

Focus on the first letter of words; for example, say the following words exaggerating the first letter:

Book   Time   Dog

Vowels help to produce a nice sound; look at the letters in the box below:

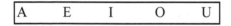

A   E   I   O   U

The vowels allow your voice to flow naturally and give you the best opportunity to sound your best.

It is helpful to learn to recognise words, which are easy to sing and those, which are not.

Hard Words To Sing

It's a great idea to understand which sounds are easy to sing and which are not; for example, words containing 'er' sounds (such as the word 'where') are difficult to sing, this is because of the 'er' sound in the middle of the word. Many words contain this sound; see if you can think of some. Here are some examples:

Hard words to sing:

There Share Care

It is also important to note that these 'hard words' are very difficult to sing high, in fact the higher you sing the harder they become. The more you practise them the easier they will become; however, they may always feel a little uncomfortable, even for professional singers.

Easy Words To Sing

Easy words are any words containing 'ah' sounds, (such as 'far'). There are lots of words that make this sound. When you sing some words they sound different to when they are spoken, this is because when you sing these words you stretch the middle part of the word and this produces the 'ah' sound. Here are some examples below:

Easy words to sing:

Car Love Fun Sun

Exercise 2.

The natural progression after humming is to open your mouth and sing 'Ah'.

Hum a note that feels comfortable and then, still humming, open your mouth and sing 'Ah'. It will sound like 'Mah': remember to open your mouth wide.

If your mouth is opening the same amount as if you were speaking, then you need to open much wider. Remember that singing and speaking are different; don't sing in the same way that you speak!

Exercise 3.

Try singing 'Mah' at different levels in your voice; for example, higher and lower.

The higher you sing, the wider you need to open your mouth.

The following exercises are great to practise, as they will help your voice warm up before singing songs.

Exercise 4.

Sing other sounds such as 'Mee' and 'Moo'. Sing on a note in your voice that feels comfortable; for example, not too high or low and hold the note for as long or short as you like.

Exercise 5.

Make your own combinations by adding different consonants or sing the examples in the boxes below:

Hold the notes for as long as you can with your mouth open wide; however, don't hold it so long that you uncomfortably run out of breath.

Mah	Mee	Moo

Vah	Vee	Kah	Dah	Dee	Doo

Remember to practise the above whilst standing and breathing correctly, with your face 'lifted' and sing on a note that is comfortable for you.

There are two different sounds in singing; 'open sounds' and 'closed sounds'. Look at the examples in the boxes below:

'Open sound'

ah

Open sounds are easy to sing, 'ah' is an open sound because your mouth is open wide and therefore it is easier to sing.

'Closed sounds'

e and o

Closed sounds are hard to sing, 'e' and 'o' are closed and difficult because your mouth is barely open.

Summary of singing with words:
Exaggerate consonants and sing them quickly.
Sing through the vowels and hold them for as long as the word will allow.
Learn to recognise which words are easy and which are best to avoid if possible.

Recommended daily practice: 5-10 minutes no more than five days a week.
Limit this for young children to two days a week.

In the next lesson, you will practise singing complete songs.

Lesson Six:
Singing Songs

In this lesson, you will utilise all the techniques (good habits) you have learnt in the previous lessons and apply them to songs. One of the most important skills to embrace is to learn to exaggerate the words in songs.

Exaggerating the words will help your singing in so many ways, it can have an immediate effect on your sound, which will become louder and clearer. Regardless of your ability, you will definitely improve and begin to sound more professional, you will even look and sound like 'a singer'!

Exercise 1.
Sing a song of your choice and exaggerate all the words. It may feel strange at first, but remember singing and speaking are different, and it will take a while to get used to.

Put your favourite song on the CD player and sing along, working hard to accentuate all the words. It is important to note: it can take time to get to know the sound of your own voice.

Go for it!
Don't be shy!

In order to hear yourself better, there is a simple trick: put your hand over your ear and you will sound twice as loud to yourself.

Exercise 2.

Looking in your mirror – using your new 'good habits' – stand correctly, check your posture, take a deep breath (making sure your chest rises) and lift your face with a smile. Sing your chosen song and exaggerate all the words, making sure you open your mouth wider than when you speak.

Also remember to lift your face with each breath you take.

Checklist to remember:

Stand correctly.

Take a deep breath through your mouth and lift your chest.

Smile, look surprised and lift your eyebrows.

Exaggerate all the words.

Open your mouth wider.

If you are finding it difficult to incorporate all of these at once, don't worry; just practise a couple of them at any one time. It will still make a big difference to your voice.

TOP TIP

Record yourself singing it's a great way to hear your progress.

42

Reaching the high notes

It is completely normal to find singing higher notes more difficult. No matter whether your voice sits naturally high or low, the high sections of some songs can be very hard. I have a few tips that can help: some singers stand on tiptoes or lift their chin up hoping this might make it easier; unfortunately, this will not work.

However, there are a couple of things, which, if practised, over time will help. Firstly, open your mouth wider the higher you go; secondly, lift your eyebrows and face with maximum effort. The more effort you put in the easier it will become. Another good tip is to change the way you think, try to imagine the notes are not going up, but are horizontal, as if you are walking in a straight line. Remember you have to use your imagination because you can't see your voice. Even try to convince yourself the song is getting lower instead of higher.

Remember, it may not be your voice that's having the problem with the high notes; it may be because your song contains 'closed sounds'. In this case, change the word to an 'ah' sound; this is a technique professional singers use. Above all, try not to get frustrated; even professional singers have to work hard to overcome such difficulties.

TOP TIP

Always sing reasonably loudly when singing high, it's much easier to reach the notes.

Song Choices

There are many different styles of songs, some easier to sing than others, from pop, rock, jazz, R&B, musicals and classical, each have their own challenges. It's not just the style that needs consideration, but also the language, as much as there are songs in English, there are equally many songs in different languages, especially in classical songs such as opera. Some languages are easier than others; for example, Italian is easier than English due to the many vowel sounds; however, most singers find their first language easier to sing.

Some voices are more suited to a certain style, for example, you may be really good at singing classical songs, but rock songs may be a challenge; you may find singing rock songs easy, but can't sing musical theatre. Some people will find it easier than others to sing different styles, but no one can sing everything. Some styles are more relaxed, such as pop, rock, jazz and R&B, musical theatre and classical can be a little strict and technical. Focus on the style you enjoy singing; however, it can be fun to try something else, so if you're a pop diva give a classical number a go! You may find you have a hidden talent!

Some people find singing fast songs easier than slow ones and vice versa.

Singing Fast Songs

Fast songs are much easier to sing when you are nervous, so if you are entering your first karaoke competition or auditioning for the local choir, pick a fast song, as it's easier to hide the nerves. Fast songs will also hide imperfections in the voice such as tuning problems due to much shorter phrases. The disadvantage with fast songs can be the breathing – it is harder to find a place to breathe – try to snatch a quick breath whenever you can; it may not be in the perfect place, but you may not have a choice and because the song is moving fast no one will really notice. There is no time to take large breaths so little ones more often are fine. Fast songs can also feel hard sometimes if there are lots of words. Singing some fast songs may feel as if you have never spoken so quickly and this can feel strange. The rule with singing is to keep your mouth open, wider than when you speak. There is one exception to this, when singing lots of fast words, there is simply no time to achieve this. This is the only occasion when you open your mouth significantly less whilst singing.

Helpful Tips For Singing Fast Songs

Take quick small breaths whenever possible.

Don't open your mouth too wide when singing lots of fast words as there isn't enough time.

Practise the difficult sections you find harder more often.

Singing Slow Songs

Slow songs can be much harder to sing than fast ones, this is due to long notes you may need to hold. Such songs will show all the imperfections in the voice, in particular the tuning and breath control. However, some things are so much easier such as the breathing; yes, holding the long notes may be difficult, but there are many more places to breathe and there is time to decide when to take a breath. If you take a big breath before a long note, but feel you won't make it to the end, simply cut the long note short. It can also be very exhausting holding all the long notes to the bitter end and your singing will suffer!

Helpful Tips For Singing Slow Songs

Cut the long notes shorter.

Think in advance when to breathe.

Practise the difficult sections you find harder more often.

There are also other factors to consider with songs, it's not just the style of a song that can make it difficult and challenging; for example, singing a high note in a pop song is just as testing as singing a high note in a classical song. Also, singing unaccompanied (singing alone without a backing track or any music in the background) can be very difficult for some singers as it's much harder to stay in tune and keep the song flowing. However, it's good to practise sections of the song without any music as you can really hear yourself. Other aggravating factors which can be annoying, are things such as the need to swallow, cough or clear your throat. This is normal and natural so don't worry, simply cut a note short so you can deal with these issues. Remember, it's your body that's doing the work so these things will happen; don't hang on till the bitter end of the song to sort out the problem or you won't be able to enjoy your song.

Recommended daily practice: 15-20 minutes, or for as long as you feel comfortable but not for more than five days a week. Reduce this for children.

Lesson Seven:
Confidence and Self-Criticism

Confidence

When singing, a lack of confidence can be a battle, good singing is 50% confidence and 50% technique. Singing is personal and can be embarrassing; this is partly due to the fact it's your own body that makes the sound. If you play an instrument, you probably feel more confident, even if you're not very good. This is because the sound is coming from something other than you; when singing, YOU are the instrument!

The more you sing, the better your confidence will become; in fact, learning to sing can actually help to build your confidence in other areas of your life. I once had a friend who lacked self-confidence and found it difficult to speak in public, which was an integral part of her job, so I advised her to take singing lessons. The singing lessons she received gave her the confidence she needed, and her ability and newfound self-belief increased, as such her ability to speak in public became less of a trauma.

It's easy to sing in your bedroom or in the shower where no one can hear you, but it is much more challenging to sing on a stage in front of an audience. All your barriers and defence mechanisms 'pop up'! The most common of these is to sing quieter but, if you lose your sound, your technique disappears (singing quietly is so hard that it requires application). Your breathing will become shallow and your diction poor, overall you will start to sound terrible and your self-esteem will plummet! It's all because your confidence has gone.

Always try to practise in a comfortable environment where you feel relaxed, it is also important you choose a place where you can sing loudly so that you can gain maximum benefit.

TOP TIP

Sing with a friend who is also learning to sing. This will help your confidence grow.

It can be difficult to sing in front of friends and family; singing to people you know is often worse than singing to strangers! If you would like to try performing, why not take part in a karaoke night, especially if it is in a place where no one knows you, such as on holiday or at a pub; the more you perform, the better your confidence will become. Another great way to perform is to join a local singing group, such as a choir or musical theatre club where you could join the chorus; if your dream is to sing with a band, try being part of the backing group to support a lead vocalist.

It's a great idea to sing with a group of people who are also learning, it could be with your classmates at school, with friends or family at home, or colleagues at work. This will help your confidence and can also be really enjoyable as well as good fun.

Remember, even those with amazing singing voices can lack confidence.

Performing as part of a group of singers will help you to blend in; your confidence will grow.

Self-Criticism

It is important to become familiar with the sound of your own voice and to have realistic expectations. You may never sound like Pavarotti or Whitney Houston, but remember they will never sound like you either! Don't forget, everyone's voice is unique and individual.

It is not uncommon after two lessons to feel disappointed and think: 'Why don't I sound like a famous performer?' Don't worry; it definitely takes longer than two lessons to improve!

It is important to recognise that whilst self-criticism can be a useful tool it can also be something which can have a negative effect. You must not become impatient and angry with yourself, as it will not achieve anything. Remember that learning all the 'good habits' can take time, if you are having difficulty with one thing then try not to focus on it, move on to something else and in time everything will fall into place.

You will improve to a level within your own natural range of ability and capability, some will have the potential to experience a dramatic improvement and might even want to start applying for talent shows and other competitions; for others, it's a slower process, you may never sound like a professional performer or a famous 'pop diva', but you will improve on a personal level and within your ability and that is something of which you can be very proud of.

Know your limits and be realistic.

Lesson Eight:
Do's and Don'ts

The Do's

• Warming up is an important part of your daily singing routine. Before you start singing, you must take a couple of minutes to do this. (Choose your favourite exercises from lessons 4 and 5.)

• Practise singing songs you know well as the body uses muscle memory for singing, so your old favourites will be easier. Singing a new song will feel difficult and a bit more of a challenge at first; sing it as much as possible and, in time, it will feel more comfortable.

- If you are intending to sing in the morning, you must eat breakfast. Singing can be very energetic and coupled with the deep breathing can make you feel faint, leave approximately 30 minutes between eating and singing.

- Singing with a head cold, which has not progressed onto your chest is fine; however, avoid singing when you have a sore throat, as this will just aggravate how ill you feel and make you feel worse. A slightly blocked nose gives a nice resonant sound and can help to 'place' the voice – this means focusing your voice to achieve a better tone.

The Don'ts

- One of the biggest contributors to vocal problems is talking; many think it's smoking, but this is not the case. Talking for protracted periods of time, especially late at night, can strain the vocal cords and cause a husky uncomfortable feeling whilst singing. For example, if you spend an evening with friends chatting away till late, the following day you will find it hard to sing; if you want to keep your voice in good condition, beware and look after it!

- If you have a performance, it is better to go to bed early the night before and avoid a late night, if possible; your voice will always sound better if you have had a good nights sleep.

- As a result of over-practising, you can do more damage than good. Undertaking 10 minutes of focused technical practise, is better than 2 hours of blasting out your favourite tunes. A good balance is 10 minutes of technical warm-up and 30 minutes singing songs; always take two days off a week and avoid singing late in the evening. Rest is very good for the voice and when your body is tired, this can be reflected on how you sound and perform. The majority of well-known instruments played by musicians and performers require hours of daily practice, but this simply isn't the case with singing.

- If you are a parent and studying this book with young children under 10 years of age, limit vocal exercises to a few minutes each day, four days a week followed by singing fun songs for a further 10-15 minutes; keep breathing exercises to a minimum.

Frequently Asked Questions

How do I know if I have a high or low voice?

Whether you are a 'high' or 'low' singer is determined by where your voice sits comfortably, not whether you can sing some really high notes or some really low notes. If you are a 'low' singer, you may still reach the high notes, but you won't be able to remain high for any length of time and your voice will give up, needing to drop low again. It's the same for 'high' singers; you will have low notes in your vocal range, but you won't want to sing the low notes for long!

I am a boy and my voice is breaking, can I still learn to sing?

Yes, but it will be unpredictable, be patient and expect the unexpected! You would have had a high voice, like a choirboy, before your voice started to break and change. Now you have no idea where it will be, practise the exercises in this book and over time, your new voice will be revealed! It can take anything from a year to five years for your voice to settle.

I am pregnant, can I still sing?

Yes, up to a point, and it can be really good for you. Singing will keep you fit and active and will help your posture. Breathing exercises can be helpful for childbirth and building your stamina. After 6 months or so, you may feel a little uncomfortable, so gentle singing is the best way forward.

I am 70 years old; can I still improve my voice?

Yes, anyone at any age can improve their voice, you may find progress slower and not as effective, the breathing, lifting and posture exercises will keep you in great shape. However, be careful not to put too much strain on your body, be realistic and know your limits.

Can young children learn to sing?

Yes, but it must be very limited. Young children are not physically ready to undertake the rigorous training of someone in their late teens. They will also have difficulty singing in tune, which is completely normal, but this will not remain the case in adulthood. Keep breathing exercises to a minimum, or not at all, instead, focus more on smiling and humming. Above all, make it fun and try to include clapping and dancing whilst singing, training can become more technical for the age group 12-15, but still be cautious in your approach.

Will alcohol affect my voice?

Yes, it can. Beware of drinking too much alcohol as it can dry out your voice and make singing feel uncomfortable and hard work.

Can dairy products damage my voice?

No, but they can make your throat feel sticky and uncomfortable; it is best to avoid them if you have a performance.

Is it true that you need to be of a larger build to be an opera singer?

No, this is not true. Years ago, it was almost expected that to be an opera singer you had to be of a larger build, this is a myth! It's much better to be of a healthy weight; in fact, some opera singers are of petite build but have the same if not more stamina. Your size has nothing to do with your vocal power or quality; if you are very underweight through malnutrition, your power and voice in general will suffer. If you are overweight, your voice will still be good, but your breathing and stamina may not!

I become so nervous if I have to sing in public, is there anything that can help?

The first thing you must realise is that becoming nervous is quite normal, everyone feels this way before a performance; it is essential to learn how to control and manage your nerves so that they don't affect your singing voice. There are different levels of feeling nervous, some individuals are able to control it whereas others feel a mixture of nerves and excitement, and for some it's completely uncontrollable to the point where they actually feel physically sick. The more occasions you perform, the easier it will be to be able to control your nerves and tension; you have to become familiar with how your body reacts to nerves and then you can take steps to control it.

Here are a few tips:

Taking big breaths before you sing can help to calm you down.

Make sure you have eaten properly a few hours before (a low sugar level will just make your nerves worse).

Perform as much as possible and it will become easier. Also, you will find that a longer performance will give you the chance to become familiar with both your surroundings and your audience, you will feel more comfortable and be able to settle into your performance.

Make sure that you know your performance songs really well; if you are uncertain of the words or a section of the song is unclear to you, your nerves are more likely to impact on how you feel and your singing. It is easier for beginners to perform with a copy of the words to the songs, either by holding them or resting them on a stand. This can feel like a great comfort but try to look up at times above the heads of the audience; eye contact with audience members can be very off-putting for an inexperienced performer.

Nerves can be unpredictable, you may feel trepidation days before a performance, but when you come to perform these nerves may disappear. It can also be the other way round, you may have no nerves at all before walking out on stage, then when you begin your performance you suddenly feel the anxiety of the occasion.

Remember, even famous singers and performers suffer from nerves before and during a performance.

Why does my mouth sometimes feel dry before I sing and drinking water makes it drier?

This problem is associated with nerves; don't worry about this, it is quite normal. Try sucking a cough sweet or a strong mint, it does actually work wonders! However, avoid brightly coloured sweets as they stain the tongue: you don't want a 'rainbow' inside your mouth when you open your mouth to sing!

What does tone-deaf mean?

Tone-deaf means you cannot sing in tune or pitch a note correctly. It does not mean you have a terrible voice and can't sing – there is nothing wrong with the vocal cords – it has to do with hearing the music and not being able to process it correctly.

Despite many people thinking that they suffer with this, in fact very few people really are tone-deaf; it's actually pretty rare and can be overcome by listening more carefully to the tune or notes. Hum the notes before singing them and listen carefully to find the correct pitch. It will be a slow process but, over time, it will improve. So if you think you may be tone-deaf, do not let it affect your enjoyment of singing.

I feel like I have a break in the middle of my voice. It also sounds as if I have two different singing voices, one is low and loud; the other is high and quiet?

The voice is split into two distinct places; head voice and chest voice. Chest voice is low and loud and is great for 'belting' out pop songs and musical theatre songs; the head voice will sound gentle and quieter. Opera singers however, can have a very loud head voice and chest voice.

There is also a break between the two voices, this can be a problem and some singers may feel that they 'get stuck'; others will sing over the break with ease and some will not feel the break at all. High singers tend to sit in the head voice (some have a high belt voice) lower singers, however, will find the break more of a problem which can make it sometimes harder to overcome.

Every voice is different; therefore there is no right or wrong place for the 'break' to sit. Regular singing around the 'break' will help you to improve – start low and go up 'flipping' over into your head voice, it can sound messy but over time will iron out.

I would like singing lessons. How do I find a good teacher?

One of the best ways to find a reputable and professional singing teacher can be by way of 'word of mouth'; ask friends, work colleagues and associates if they know of anyone. Teachers also advertise in local papers and on social media, there are also music shops in some local high streets; the staff should have a list of local teachers and may be able to advise you.

If you are female, a teacher of the same gender may be better and vice versa for men. However, it doesn't really matter as long as you are comfortable with the teacher. When you arrange your first lesson, ask where your teacher studied and which qualifications he or she has attained.

Qualifications to look out for include:
Degree in music (BMus)
Diploma in vocal teaching (Dip)
Singing exams (the highest grade is 8)

There are several music exam boards, including: Associated Board of the Royal Schools of Music (ABRSM), Trinity College London and London College of Music (LCM).

A good singing teacher will be able to prepare you properly and appropriately for these exams and enter you for these, which take place approximately three times a year and are available wordwide.

How much can singing lessons cost?

Most private teachers will charge at a starting hourly rate of between £20-40 per hour. This amount can increase upwards of £60 per hour in the more expensive areas, predominantly London and major cities. Primarily, the majority of teachers will also offer more affordable 30-minute lessons, although you might consider taking a lesson every other week or once a month in order to keep the costs affordable. It is important to note that lessons for children under 10 years of age should be no longer than 20-30 minutes.

Singing as a Career

A career in singing can depend on three main things; talent, training and luck, some singers believe if you simply have the talent you will have a career; this is not the case. In a perfect world, this is how it should be, but in reality, things are quite different.

A career in singing depends on other factors, which cannot be controlled such as luck and money. Becoming a singer is similar to starting your own business; you have to put money in to get money out! Money can help with your promotion in your chosen career path, it will assist with photographs, a 'demo' recording, and if it is opera, you will need a multitude of qualifications, all of which can be very expensive. A lot of singers have to have a second job to support their singing career in the early stages of 'breaking through'.

The requirements for each type of singing career are different; I will discuss these each in turn, and offer advice regarding what you will need in order to be successful.

Pop Singer

There are so many styles of pop singing, from rock and pop to dance and R&B, whether you want to be a solo performer or a band member, the requirements are similar. As well as a good image, you will need a demo recording, without these two essential elements, finding work will be difficult – image can have more impact on your success than your voice!

Most singers will start performing in clubs and small venues, eventually building a foundation and reputation to take things to the next level, which would be sending your demos and publicity to various recording companies. Another great way to build your reputation is to develop a fan base using social media and the internet.

Take part in competitions, from karaoke to talent shows, many can be found advertised in local and national newspapers, music magazines and on the internet. For those who feel courageous, there are also the famous talent shows on TV!

Look out for auditions – there are so many, from boy band members to rock bands, the more auditions you participate in, the better your chances and opportunities. It is normal to feel disappointment if you're unsuccessful, don't become despondent as each audition is an invaluable experience. Of course, it would be helpful to be part of a well-known family, or to be promoted by someone who has money to invest in your career, but there are very few lucky enough to find themselves in this position. Being in the right place at the right time can make your career, perform whenever the opportunity arises and never turn down a 'gig', as it could be the most important one of your life.

There are also a number of international qualifications available in popular music. If you want to study at home or with a private teacher and gain some qualifications, you can take Rockschool or Trinity Rock & Pop exams, these are graded 1 to 8 and are available in most instruments associated with pop music, including vocals.

Another route would be to study popular music at a college, university or contemporary music school. There are many courses available offering diplomas, a music technology degree or a contemporary music degree. However, it should be noted that to be able to access higher education in this field, you might require a number of specific qualifications.

Musical Theatre Singer

A career in musical theatre can partly depend upon where you trained. For example, most musical singers will have studied at a performing arts college or stage school and will have studied singing, dancing and drama. Some stage schools place an emphasis on singing, whereas others are more dance-orientated.

Entry to these schools and colleges is usually by way of audition, which you will be expected to pay for, so be careful where you choose. For example, if you have never danced, avoid certain stage schools, as they may require high grades in ballet (read the prospectuses carefully).

It is possible to break into musical theatre without any formal training, some West End shows, or cruise ships hold open auditions, which means anyone can apply; however, this can be a challenging and tough route, that being said, it is by no means impossible.

Stage school applicants are generally aged from 16-21; the best age to start your training is 18. Most singing based stage schools would prefer applicants with singing exams, although it's not an official requirement, your local singing teacher will be able to provide you with the training and guidance preparing you for the exams. As well as singing exams, experience in drama and dance will also be welcomed. A-levels or equivalent qualifications will not be necessary, unless your preferred course includes a degree. Stage schools can be expensive; however, scholarships are available and information regarding these can be obtained from the respective schools.

Opera Singer

Training to become an opera singer is the longest and most intensive of all the singing styles. Talent is an essential requirement and as with all music careers, an element of luck will also play a part. Without the talent, there is no career; you need to have a powerful voice, coupled with natural control and vibrato – a good ear for music and languages is also helpful. Intense training normally begins around the age of  18-21 at a music college, or a good university. Training can continue until your early thirties as the voice matures with age. Most opera singers will have a diploma or degree in music.

Although full-time training does not start until you go to a music college or university, you will need to have studied music and singing to a high level prior to auditioning.

Entry requirements may include singing, theory and piano exams, A-level Music or equivalent qualifications.

A career in classical singing embraces several different styles, these include opera, oratorio, art song and contemporary works; each of these styles can be sung in any language, but the most popular would be English, French, German, Italian, Spanish and Latin. During training, you will study singing in foreign languages; but you will not be required to learn to speak these languages or become fluent in any of them.

Most opera singers will also teach during some point in their career, whether it be on a private basis or at a university or music college. The most successful singers will provide masterclasses at the most prestigious and well-known centres of musical excellence.

Singing Vocabulary

Professional singers use technical terms to describe different types of voices and singing, if you have heard of them before you might like to know what they mean.

SOPRANO: Female singer who has a high voice.

MEZZO-SOPRANO: Female singer who has a medium to high voice.

CONTRALTO: Female singer who has a low voice.

COUNTERTENOR: Male singer who has a high voice, he will have the same sound as the mezzo-soprano or alto and will join the female section in a choir. He will have a woman's voice when singing but his speaking voice will be within the normal range for a man.

TENOR: Male singer who has a high voice.

BARITONE: Male singer who has a mid-range voice.

BASS: Male singer who has a low voice.

INTONATION: Voice tuning; singing in tune or out of tune.

TESSITURA: Where your voice sits, for example, either high or low.

VIBRATO: The natural 'wobble' in the voice, this tends to happen at the end of longer notes. Opera singers have a strong vibrato.

A CAPPELLA: To sing unaccompanied with no instruments or backing track.

DICTION: A clear pronunciation so that every letter of every word can be heard properly.